Power for the Journey

Inspiration and Empowerment for Your Breast Cancer Journey

Caretha Crawford

This product is available at special quantity discounts for bulk purchase.

For details, write soallmayknow@gmail.com

Power for the Journey by Caretha Crawford, D. Min.

So**A**ll**M**ay**K**now Publishing

P O Box 6718

Largo, MD 20792

Soallmayknow@gmail.com

This book or parts thereof may not be reproduced in any form, stored in a retrieval system, or transmitted in any form by any means—electronic, mechanical, photocopy, recording, or otherwise—without permission of the publisher, except as provided by the United States of America copyright law.

Unless otherwise noted, all Scripture quotations are from the New King James Version of the Bible. Copyright ©1979, 1980, 1982 by Thomas Nelson, Inc., publishers. Used by permission.

Scripture quotations marked KJV are from the King James Version of the Bible.

Copyright © 2024 by Caretha Crawford

All rights reserved.

Cover designed by Caretha Franks Crawford

Author Back Cover Photo: Michael Davis

ISBN 978-1-7347064-8-2 (print)

Library of Congress Control Number: 2024901737

Visit authors website: drcarethacrawford@gmail.com

While the author has made every effort to provide accurate internet addresses at the time of publication, neither the publisher nor the author assumes any responsibility for errors or for changes that occur after publication. Further, the publisher does not have any control over and does not assume any responsibility for author of third-party websites or their content.

Printed in the United States of America

This booklet is dedicated to my niece, Ashleigh, who is fighting a winning battle. By the grace of God and a fierce attitude, she is an OVERCOMER!

Contents

Foreword	ix
Introduction	xi
Chapter 1	1
Chapter 2	9
Chapter 3	15
About the Author	19
Also by Caretha Crawford	25

Foreword

An adage says, "A picture is worth a thousand words." Whether that statement is true or not is debatable. However, what I know is accurate and not debatable is that Dr. Caretha Crawford has provided more than a thousand words for her readers that will encourage and inspire those who take the time to read and meditate on this booklet, ***Power for the Journey***. Dr. Caretha Crawford has always been a champion for women, but in this booklet, she takes her gloves off and goes toe to toe to battle with women seeking to overcome breast cancer.

She encourages women to wage war with the enemy by suiting up with God's spiritual gear, wielding the word of God, the strongest and most powerful weapon anyone can carry. I do not doubt that with this booklet embedded in your spirit, a manifestation of healing is on the way.

Dr. Gloria Miller Perrin
A Survivor/Thriver

Introduction

October is breast cancer awareness month; this is a good thing; however, women are diagnosed with breast cancer 365 days a year. Women diagnosed during months other than October need encouragement when newly diagnosed. This booklet is a quick reference for anyone needing immediate inspiration and encouragement when they first hear the words "It's cancer" and also during their breast cancer journey. It's an easy-to-read faith-builder small enough to carry in a pocket or purse.

Even though the information presented in this booklet is biblically based, it shouldn't replace health care and medical science. Instead, use it in conjunction with the advice of your healthcare providers. God is the Healer. He sometimes uses those that He has given scientific and medical knowledge to aid in the healing process.

Nothing is more powerful than God's Word. It's the best remedy for this dreaded disease. "He sent His Word and **healed** them..." (Psalm 107:20). God's Word is our spiritual medicine.

We are healed from the inside out. Restoring the spirit rebuilds the body. When we ingest Scripture as prescribed, it strengthens and restores the body, mind, and spirit. We must believe and regularly apply God's Word to our situation to realize our healing.

This booklet, *Power for the Journey*, presents relevant scriptures, confessions, affirmations, and prayers to strengthen those seeking to overcome breast cancer. Take a daily dose of God's medicine, stand firm in the faith, and hold on until you see the manifestation of your healing.

Chapter 1

Empowered For Battle

Women in the kingdom of God are invested with great power, more than most of us realize. According to Romans 8:11, the same Spirit that raised Jesus from the dead lives in us—that's power beyond measure. This power is available to us 24/7. We can walk in and wield this power on demand, especially during times of crisis, difficulties, and uncertainties.

The enemy knows how strong and powerful women are. So, he attacks us, hoping to diminish our physical strength and our mental resolve. His goal is to wear us down and render us powerless and useless.

There is no other time in history that God has used His women like the present. It's the Black woman's time and turn. We have been mistreated and oppressed throughout the generations, enduring racism, sexism, and cultural biases. God has released us for such a time as this as a mighty army against the kingdom of darkness. Therefore, we have become more of a threat to and target of the enemy. He battles for our minds, emotions, spirits, and bodies. But thanks be to God, who has given us authority over all the power of the wicked one; we don't have to become a casualty of war.

God purposefully placed enmity between Satan's seed and the woman's Seed. Enmity is deep-seated hatred or hostility. The woman has a special place and role in God's end-time plan. She gives birth and is a nourisher. The woman's seed is nourished through her breast. Sustenance for life comes from her bosom. Satan is still trying to destroy the woman and her seed by cutting off the life source.

Even though the enemy attacks us in the natural realm, we don't engage the enemy in the natural. My mother often said, "Your flesh is no match for the devil." If we are going to win the battle, we must wage war in the spirit.

Ephesians 6 commands us to *be strong in the Lord and the power of His might*. To be strong denotes to be *capable, to have the ability, to be empowered, and strengthened*. To be effective in warfare, we must suit up with God's spiritual gear—the whole armor of God.

> *Therefore take up the whole armor of God, that you may be able to withstand in the evil day, and having done all, to stand. Stand therefore, having girded your waist with truth, having put on the breastplate of right-*

eousness, and having shod your feet with the preparation of the gospel of peace; above all, taking the shield of faith with which you will be able to quench all the fiery darts of the wicked one. And take the helmet of salvation, and the sword of the Spirit, which is the word of God; praying always with all prayer and supplication in the Spirit, being watchful to this end with all perseverance and supplication for all the saints—

Ephesians 6:13-18

Lions Gird with Truth

We must gird our lions with TRUTH. Gird means to prepare for a difficult or challenging task. Why truth? It holds the other parts of the armor securely in place. Truth defeats the enemy. He has nothing to expose or use to his advantage when we are transparent and operate with integrity. God desires truth in the inward parts. When we are truthful, there are no hindrances between us and God, our Healer. If you know your life has weaknesses and temptations, confess it and close the door on the enemy.

Breast Plate Of Righteousness

The breastplate of righteousness covers the vital organs, such as the heart and lungs. Righteousness says we are in right relationship with God—made righteous by the blood of Jesus. Knowing that we have favor with God allows us to stand in assurance and declare that nothing deadly can overpower or overtake us.

Feet Shod with the Preparation of the Gospel of Peace

When we shod our feet in the Gospel of peace, we stand sure-footed, anchored, secure, stable, and unmovable from what we know to be true. There is nothing to fear because we have the peace of God or the peace which is God.

The Shield of Faith

The shield of faith protects us from doubt and unbelief. We can go into battle trusting God's promises and believing He is with us and for us. When we pick up our shield, which is faith, the enemy's darts are of no avail.

Helmet of Salvation

The helmet of salvation protects our minds and keeps our thoughts pure. The enemy desires to take possession of our minds so He can wreak havoc in our lives. Proverbs 23:7 reminds us that "For as [s]he thinks in her heart, so is [s]he." We become what we think about. The battle is to gain control of the mind.

The Sword of the Spirit

The sword of the Spirit is the Word of God. It is our offensive weapon. We must know the Word of God and speak it in faith. When we wield the Word, it's a powerful weapon against the enemy. It causes him to flee. Hebrews 4:12 states, *"For the word of God is living and powerful, and sharper than any two-edged sword, piercing even to the division of soul and spirit, and of joints and marrow, and is a discerner of the thoughts and intents of the heart."*

Pray and Pray Some More

Though prayer is not considered a piece of the armor, the armor is inadequate and ineffective without prayer. We must maintain an attitude of prayer at all times.

God has given us spiritual weapons that are effective when used as prescribed. No one has ever lost a battle using the gear in our salvation packet. As Paul stated in 1 Timothy 6:12, *"Fight the good fight of faith..."*

Command your body to align with the Word of God. Be bold, be persistent like the woman who wore down the judge in Luke 18. We must be RADICAL. Satan is relentless; therefore, we must be as well. You can't fight this battle alone. You need radical prayer warriors who will come alongside you in prayer.

Our Powerful Tongue

My sisters, God made us loquacious for a reason: let's use our mouths to wear down the enemy and build up our faith. Our words are creative and powerful. God spoke the worlds into existence. He made us in His image and according to His likeness. Therefore, we can create the world we want through obedience and with our words.

Here are a few Scriptures that remind us how powerful the tongue is:

> Death and life *are* in the power of the tongue, and those who love it will eat its fruit (Proverbs 18:21).

> There is one who speaks like the piercings of a sword, But the tongue of the wise promotes health (Proverbs 12:18).

> A wholesome tongue *is* a tree of life, but perverseness in it breaks the spirit (Proverbs 15:4).

> Pleasant words *are like* a honeycomb, sweetness to the soul and health to the bones (Proverbs 16:24).

> And the tongue *is* a fire, a world of iniquity. The tongue is so set among our members that it defiles the whole body, and sets on fire the course of nature; and it is set on fire by hell (James 3:6).

> You will also declare a thing, and it will be established for you; so light will shine on your ways (Job 22:28).

So Jesus answered and said to them, "Assuredly, I say to you, if you have faith and do not doubt, you will not only do what was done to the fig tree, but also if you say to this mountain, 'Be removed and be cast into the sea,' it will be done (Matthew 21:21).

Prayers and Affirmations

Now that you know your tongue has power, speak the following biblical affirmations and prayers over your body and situation. Declare them until they become immersed in your thinking and a part of your being. Command that your body aligns with the promises and will of God. Even though you may not feel well or see the manifestation of your healing, it doesn't nullify the Word of God that says that you are healed and made whole. We must call those things into being that have not manifested. (Romans 4:17)

Chapter 2

Who I Am

I am a child of God, purchased by His blood. He loves me with an everlasting and unconditional love.

I am the apple of God's eye. He watches over me daily and protects me from all the plots, plans, and schemes of the evil one.

I am abundantly and contagiously blessed. God provides all of my needs. He is concerned about everything that concerns me.

I am wise and forgiven. I walk in forgiveness and the wisdom of God. I keep company with the wise. I do not walk in my counsel. The Lord directs my footsteps; therefore, I never falter.

I am strong because the Lord is my strength. I will rejoice and be glad in the new mercies of each day. God satisfies my mouth with good things, and my strength is renewed like the eagles.

I am a bold and courageous warrior. God didn't give me a spirit of fear but of power, love, and a sound mind. I face each new day with gratitude and great expectations.

I am triumphant! I don't merely survive a new day; I'm thriving over all my circumstances.

I am a victor and not a victim. I'm victorious because I am an overcomer by the blood of the Lamb and the word of my testimony.

I am God's favorite child. His favor surrounds me like a shield. (Psalm 5)

I Am Healed and Made Whole

As I speak the Word of fatih to my body, mind, and spirit; body, you must align with the Word of God.

Jesus sent His word and healed me. I am delivered from all my destructions, from the enemy, the world, and my flesh. (Psalm 107:20)

I am loaded daily with God's benefits. They are activated in my life and are fulfilling their purposes. Healing is one of my benefits; therefore, no sicknesses nor diseases will triumph in my body. (Psalm 68:19, Psalm 103:2; Jeremiah 17:14)

Jesus bore my pain and took my sicknesses. Therefore, I am pain and disease-free. (Isaiah 53:4)

Because the life of the Living God lives in me, growths and tumors cannot exist in my body. The life blood of Jesus dissolved and eradicated them. (Lev. 17:11; John 10:10)

Every organ of my body is healthy and functions the way God designed it to function—my red and white blood cells are in proper balance. (Jeremiah 30:17)

The Spirit that raised Jesus from the dead lives in me; therefore, my immune system is strong and wards off all viruses and illnesses that attempt to invade my body. (Romans 8:11)

I am whole and walking in good health. The healing anointing of Jesus runs through my body day and night. It eradicates anything that tries to traffic in my body, mind, and spirit illegally. By the stripes of Jesus, I am healed. He is the God who heals me. (Isaiah 53:5; 1 Peter 2:24)

I am whole, mind, body, and spirit. I will live my full days in peace, health, and prosperity. My spirit is strong, and it sustains me. (1 Thessalonians 5:23; Proverbs 18:14)

I think good thoughts. Positive thoughts. Godly thoughts. I think on those things that are true, honest, just, pure, lovely, and of a good report. And as I think, so do I become. (Philippians 4:8; Proverbs 23:7)

I am redeemed from all past, present, and future curses. Affliction will not arise a second time. (Galatians 3:13; Nahum 1:9)

My faith in God and knowledge of Him increase daily. It's my faith that has made me whole. I will not meditate on or believe the lies of the enemy. The enemy is a defeated foe who has no part in me. (Romans 1:17; Luke 10:19)

Medications administered to me only function to strengthen me and aid in the healing process. They will not weaken or destroy my health. (Luke 10:19)

I mediate on and praise my God and King in the night watches. I rejoice under the shadow of His wings. I commit my ways to God, and He establishes my goings and thoughts. (Psalm 63:6; Psalm 91:4; Psalm 37:5; Psalm 40:2)

God is my Restorer. Everything the enemy took from me, God is giving it back one thousandfold. (Jeremiah 30:17; Psalm 23:3; Proverbs 6:31)

The blessings of the Lord are running me down. They are making me rich, and as I water others, I am watered. I have more than enough spiritually, physically, emotionally, mentally, and financially to live on and share with others. (Deut. 28:2; Psalm 18:19; Proverbs 11:25; John 10:10)

God hides me from the secret plots of the enemy. Under His wings, I find refuge. He is my strong tower. ((Psalm 31:20, 64:2, 61:3, 91:2, 4; Proverbs 18:10)

No weapon formed against me shall prosper and every word spoken against me shall be condemned. (Isaiah 54:17)

Every promise God has made to me will come to fruition. My destiny is life, healing, and health. (2 Corinthians 1:20; John 10:10)

Jesus is my hope for each new day. I will always depend on Him to have my back and fight my battles. He hears my cries and attends to my prayers. When my heart is overwhelmed, He leads me to the Rock that is higher than I. (Lamentations 3:24; 2 Chronicles 20:17; Psalm 40:1, 61:2)

God is my constant companion. He promised me: When you pass through the waters, I will be with you; and through the rivers, they shall not overflow you. When you walk through the fire, you shall not be burned, nor shall the flame scorch you. (Isaiah 43:2)

I will live and not die and declare the works of the Lord. (Psalm 118:17)

This is the report of the Lord. I believe it and embrace it.

It's the Lord's doings, and it's marvelous in my eyes!

God has given me beauty for ashes (Isaiah 61:3).

Chapter 3

Don't Give Up

Remember. Sisters, you are stronger than you think. You have more power in your pinky finger than the enemy possesses. Because God has given us "...power to tread on serpents and scorpions and over all the power of the enemy: and nothing shall by any means hurt you" (Luke 10:19 KJV).

Don't listen to the lies of the enemy. "Submit yourselves therefore to God. Resist the devil, and he will flee from you" (James 4:7 KJV).

Don't grow weary. "And let us not grow weary while doing good, for in due season we shall reap if we do not lose heart" (Galatians 6:9).

. . .

Allow Proverbs 3:5 to be a reality in your life. "Trust in the Lord with all thine heart; and lean not unto thine own understanding" (Proverbs 3:5). This verse should be more than your favorite verse on a mug or plaque. It should be inscribed on your heart.

Do seek medical advice. God married medical science and the faith community. There is nothing new under the sun. The author of 1 Chronicles states, "For all things come from You, and from Your hand we have given to You." Medical knowledge comes from God. Jesus commingled the medical community and faith. He told the ten lepers, "Go show yourselves to the priest." The priest in that day gave oversight to the medical community. (Luke 17:14)

Enlist the help of others. "Confess your trespasses to one another, and pray for one another, that you may be healed. The effective, fervent prayer of a righteous [wo]man avails much" (James 5:16). "Two are better than one, because they have a good reward for their labor" (Ecclesiastes 4:9).

Maintain your joy. "...Do not sorrow, for the joy of the Lord is your strength" (Nehemiah 8:10). "A merry heart does good, *like* medicine, but a broken spirit dries the bones" (Proverbs 17:22).

. . .

Do read and say the thoughts in this booklet out loud so that they will penetrate your being and ward off the contrary thoughts that will try to invade your space.

Don't Believe the Lies of the Enemy

God didn't make you sick, nor is He punishing you. God only has good things in store for His children. It's the Father's good pleasure to give you the riches of the kingdom (Luke 12:32). There is no sickness in the kingdom of God.

"Beloved, I pray that you may prosper in all things and be in health, just as your soul prospers" (3 John 2).

God's Love for You

The enemy will throw darts of doubt and unbelief. He wants you to have second thoughts about whether God loves you since He allowed a disease to attack your body.

God etched you on the palms of His hands. He is carrying you. That's why you only see one set of footprints in the sand. (Isaiah 49:16)

Sister, we can turn what Satan, the enemy, meant to destroy us into something good. While you are confessing God's Word and believing for the manifestation of your healing, you are growing stronger in your faith. Your testimony will encourage others on their journey.

Prayer of Gratitude

Lord, I thank you for seeing something in me that I couldn't see in myself. You allowed me to carry a burden that I didn't know that I could carry. Thank You for Your strength that makes this challenge not only bearable, but conquerable. Jesus, thank You for the thirty-nine stripes You endured on the cross for my healing. By faith, I apply Your blood to my body and declare that I am healed and made whole in Jesus' name. Lord, I am grateful for the prayers of the righteous and the renewing of my faith. In Jesus name, Amen.

I AM AN OVERCOMER!

About the Author

I am a breast cancer OVERCOMER. I overcame this disease and not merely survived it. I am flourishing and thriving, living a victorious and vibrant life.

I was diagnosed with breast cancer on December 7, 2022. I thought I had escaped this dreaded disease even though, during her senior years, my mother was diagnosed with breast cancer. My oldest sister succumbed to the disease at the age of fifty-one. I have always been what many call a "Go-Getter" or high-functioning person. I'm constantly producing results and on the move. I have visited thirty-eight states and many countries. At seventy-three, I preach and teach the gospel with power and conviction. I am a convener of conferences and seminars and a church and worship school organizer. The worship school, In Pursuit of His Presence Worship Arts Ministries, serves as a vehicle to train liturgical dancers. I not only lead and teach others, but I am an active minister of the dance. I am an award-winning writer with eight published books to my credit. I also own a publishing and media company, **S**o**A**ll**M**ay**K**now, under which greeting cards, books, digital magazines, and films are produced.

On April 13, 2023, six days after my last radiation treatment, I was inducted into the Martin Luther King Jr. Board of Preachers at Morehouse College, Atlanta, Georgia. I'm also a mentor with The R.E.A.L. Black Women In Ministry Thrive Initiative, a 1.5 million dollar Lilly Grant mentoring organization led by Ambassador Suzan Johnson Cook.

I am a former kindergarten teacher in Maryland and a children's clothes designer. My designs have been exhibited as far as Paris, France, and sold in high-end boutiques locally and in Puerto Rico.

I am a wife and mother of one grown daughter.

I share these things with you because I want you to be encouraged and inspired by my active and productive life. There is life after breast cancer. Don't just escape the flames, but come through without the smell of smoke. You are a King's Kid (Kingdom Daughter). Romans 14:17 declares, "...for the kingdom of God is not eating and drinking, but righteousness and peace and joy in the Holy Spirit."

(Note: I wrote my life experiences in the first person to make my story less formal and more relatable.)

- facebook.com/CarethaCrawford
- instagram.com/carethacrawford
- youtube.com/@carethatv

Other Books by Caretha Franks Crawford

Promises and Prayers for Uncertain Times, a devotional is a collection of sixty Scripture verses, affirmations, and prayers, accompanied by brilliant pictures of nature. It speaks of the promises that God made to His people for challenging and uncertain times.

978-1-7347064-3-7 — $16.00

REBUILD YOUR LIFE after Spiritual Identity Theft
This book will help you retrieve your true identity. It will take you on a journey that will help you recognize the perceived limitations besetting you, the war that is going on in and around you to keep you powerless. You can write a new story!

978-1-7347064-6-8 — $15.00

Purchase on Amazon

RELAX and RECEIVE
These weekly devotional will challenge, strengthen and provide you with hope and encouragement to face each new week. Tune out this noisy world and just…Relax and Receive, the Word God has for You!

978-1-5456-3449-3 - $15.00

DETERMINED TO SUCCEED
Dr. Crawford reveals a strategic plan for women of color or any ethnic group to live a successful life. She provides practical and spiritual guidance for building your confidence so that you can get what's yours!

978-1-4984-6951-7 - $15.00

HOLD ON TO YOUR DREAM
Unfortunately, many people give up on achieving their dreams when they are faced with what seems to be insurmountable odds. Discover how to recognize and reclaim your God-given dreams, and identify steps you need to take to see your destiny fulfilled.

978-1-62136688-1- $11.00

DANCE, God's Gift to You!
Presents a fresh, clear biblical understanding of how God views the dance, elaborating on how and why dance should be used in the worship experience. This book will answer many questions and help open the eyes of your understanding to the origin and purpose of dance.

978-1-61215493-0 - $15.00

Also by Caretha Crawford

Distinguished Woman Magazine

Distinguishedwoman2020@gmail.com

www.ingramcontent.com/pod-product-compliance
Lightning Source LLC
Chambersburg PA
CBHW040639100526
44585CB00039B/2869